Halfway House Success:

A Helpful Guide for
Soon-to-be-Released Inmates

by: E. Dantes

Dedication

To my good friend RAB,
who soon will be free…

Table of Contents

Introduction

Preparing for the Streets

Halfway House: Is it Worth It?

What to Bring from Prison

Orientation

Accountability

The Pass System

Job Hunting w/ a Record

Conclusion

INTRODUCTION

Having served five years in Federal Prison, I remember there wasn't a day that went by that I didn't think about walking through those gates to freedom. One of the things that I was unsure of was what halfway house would be like.

You see, when you are an inmate, there are very few resources provided to prepare you for your transition to the outside world. I decided that this needed to change – that's why I published this little book.

In it, current inmates will gain the knowledge they need to make their halfway house experience a success.

Here is what inmates will learn:

- What they need to be doing NOW, before being released, to help them prepare for their freedom
- Factors they need to consider when deciding to take or refuse halfway house placement
- What items they need to bring with them from prison to make for an easy transition to halfway house
- Halfway house orientation – what to expect
- Accountability and how important it is to a successful halfway house experience
- The Pass System and how to navigate this often confusing process

- Subsistence – what is it and how will it affect your earnings while in halfway house
- Job hunting with a criminal record – how to navigate the job search and exactly what to say when asked about your record.

This is a guide that every inmate about to be released from prison needs to read. In addition, this book will give them the peace-of-mind to lay their course for future success as a returning citizen.

Preparing for the Streets

Okay, so you've made it almost completely through your bid and now you are getting close to going home. Here are some questions that might be on your mind:

- What should my case manager and I be discussing when I go to team to finalize my time in prison and receive my release date?
- How should I prepare myself mentally for returning to society?
- Should I take halfway house, and if so, how much time will I get?
- How difficult will it be for me to get a job now that I am considered a felon? How long will it take to adjust?

We will discuss all of these questions in this and the next few chapters.

Pace your Adjustment

Just as there was a transitional period when you went from being free to being in prison, there will be a transitional period where you will need to adjust to being free again. I remember having this idea that it would be such an easy adjustment, however, I was surprised that it was not that simple.

Depending on how much time you've served in prison, the adjustment period may be anywhere from a few months to a full year before you feel totally acclimated to your new life.

The best advice I received was from an old timer who had done several bids in both federal and state prisons. He told me to relax and take it one day at a time; there will be plenty of time to do all the things that you've missed out on. Don't try to do everything at once because you will overwhelm yourself.

You see, I had these grand plans that I was going to complete all these activities that I had been contemplating the entire time I was in prison. I love to cook and I had all these recipes that I was going to try out; all these workout routines I was going to do; classes I was going to take.

If I had rushed into all these things during the initial adjustment period, I would have been completely spent. I remembered this man's words and I decided to take it easy for the first couple of weeks.

I decided to enjoy the simple pleasures of freedom – spending time with family and friends, watching Netflix, taking a walk in nature. I realized I had plenty of time to get to all the things on "my list" – there was no rush.

Mental Preparations

There are a few things you can do while still in prison to prepare yourself mentally for going home. If you followed the advice in this book, you've created a routine for yourself in prison and made it your job.

You've kept in contact with friends and family through letters, emails, phone calls, and visits. All these people are anxiously awaiting your return and looking forward to seeing and talking to you.

You will need to prepare yourself for that because sometimes it can feel overwhelming once you are on the street, i.e. free. You'll have a cell phone that these folks will be able to call and/or text at any time during the day.

Before, you were used to using the phone in the prison where you had a fifteen-minute window to get everything out, now you can talk for as long as you want.

It might be a good idea once you get your release date to write a letter to your family and friends and let them know how much you've appreciated their love and support during your incarceration.

Tell them that you are looking forward to spending time with them and catching up, but that it is quite a transition and you might need a little time to get adjusted to normal life again.

I remember all these people called and texted me when I was released, and I felt overwhelmed because of everything else that was going on. I couldn't reach out to all of them as fast as I wanted. You have to remember, your friends and family haven't experienced what you have experienced so they won't automatically think that you'll need a little space initially to get settled in.

They're all excited for you and want to talk to you or spend time with you. It's always good to let them know ahead of time that you can't wait to reconnect, however, to ask them for a little time.

Don't get me wrong – it's going to feel wonderful to step through those gates and be on free soil, and you may need a very little adjustment period. However, from my experience and from talking to others who have made that transition, normally there is a little time and space needed to fully adjust.

Transition Team

It's important that you and your case manager are on the same page when it comes to your release. Remember that you are not the only inmate that they are responsible for; I remember that my case manager had over 175 inmates on her caseload.

There isn't an exact timeline for when they have to submit your paperwork, however I will give you some general guidelines. First, you have to decide whether you are going to take halfway house, and if so, how much time they are willing to give you there. Things change often in the B.O.P. so you will have to talk to other inmates to find out how much time others are getting.

We will discuss whether halfway house is even worth considering in the next chapter. Generally, eighteen months prior to your release date, your case manager should be discussing halfway house and your release address – that is, where you are going to live.

Some case managers will not really start any paperwork until twelve months prior to your release date. That's fine, I just wouldn't let them put it off any longer than that because I have seen guys slip through the cracks and get very little halfway house time when they needed a lot.

A good rule of thumb is to try to get six months of halfway house or home confinement. You will meet with your case manager to sign a bunch of paperwork, indicating your release address and which district your probation will be completed. They will make sure you are up-to-date on any medical requirements, like receiving a TB test within 6 months from your release.

Once all the paperwork is signed, it is submitted to the Unit Manager, then to the Warden, then off to Region, where it is processed. This is a slow and time-consuming process, that's why it's best if they start it early.

Several weeks prior to your release, you will indicate who is picking you up at the prison, or if you will require money for a bus or plane ticket. If you have no money, the B.O.P. is required to provide you with travel money, which at the time of this writing is as much as $300.

If you have any money left in your commissary account, that money will be placed on a prepaid debit card and issued to you on the date of your release. Don't be afraid to ask questions – that is what the case manager is there for, to help you transition from prison back to society.

Halfway House: Is it worth it?

This is an important chapter because for many of you, you will require halfway house to help with your transition. The question is: Is taking halfway house really worth it? That really all depends on your current situation. Here are some questions to get you thinking:

- How much money will you have on hand when you are released from prison?
- Will you have a job waiting for you when you are released or will you be unemployed?
- Do you already have a place to live, or are you homeless?
- How are your relationships with family and friends? Are they supportive or do you have some work to do to mend these relationships?

The purpose of halfway house is to help transition you from an inmate to a returning citizen. When you are a resident of the halfway house, you are still under B.O.P. custody, so you are still their responsibility.

This means you will be on a short leash until you finish your sentence. An opportunity to go to a halfway house is the B.O.P.'s way of allowing you to complete the last leg of your sentence halfway between prison and freedom. So, let's go through some of those questions to help you determine whether to take halfway house or not.

The first question is about money – how much savings do you have or will you have upon your release? Remember, you will probably be buying commissary throughout your entire sentence, which can be costly. Plus, you'll need to buy sneakers once or twice a year as well as other clothes that the B.O.P. doesn't provide.

A good rule of thumb is to budget anywhere from $1,200 - $2,400 per year in expenses while you're serving your time. If you're going to have little or no savings by the time your sentence is finished, that is one reason to consider taking the halfway house option, and pushing for as much time there as you can.

As part of the halfway house experience, you will be required to find a job, and you can even work two jobs if you need to. This is a good opportunity to work a lot and save so when you're released from halfway house, you'll have a financial cushion.

My advice: if you will have a bunch of money in savings when you are released, you have eliminated a lot of the problems that returning citizens face so you could turn down halfway house and be just fine.

If, on the other hand, you will have little or no money, I strongly recommend taking all the halfway house you can get, and pushing for the maximum when meeting with your case manager.

Next, onto employment – do you have a job waiting for you or will you need to secure employment? This is a big one. I've met many guys who had a job waiting for them when they were released from prison and so didn't have to worry about searching for a job, especially now that they carry the label of 'felon'.

If you are unemployed, again, unless you have a lot of money in savings, I would strongly recommend taking halfway house. It may take you several weeks of searching and going on job interviews before you get offered a job – I'd much rather do that while living for free at the halfway house then being fresh out of prison with rent to pay and struggling to find a job.

Housing is another important factor to consider. If you have no place to live and are technically homeless, then take the halfway house. If you are going to live with family or friends, or you have kept your own home during your incarceration, then the decision is up to you.

I would still take halfway house because if you have a place to live, you won't have to stay at the halfway house for very long before you are released to home confinement and get to live at your residence. We'll talk more about this a little later.

Finally, how are your relationships with family and friends? Do you have a lot of support from them or do you need to mend some of these relationships? The nice part about halfway house is that you will certainly have more freedom to move around and be able to meet up with and visit family and friends outside of the prison walls and the visiting room.

This can be a great opportunity to spend some quality time with your family, your spouse, and your children in a healthier environment. I know several guys that used their transitional time in halfway house to mend relationships with their children and other friends and family members.

In the next few chapters, we will delve more deeply into how halfway house works and the pluses and minuses. The thing to remember is that halfway house does suck, just not as much as prison.

Are you someone who wants to walk through that prison gate and go straight home, not having to deal with the new and different rules and regulations of a halfway house?

Or are you someone who wants to spend the least amount of time behind bars and are willing to deal with a lot of the BS of halfway house to enjoy more freedom and time with loved ones?

You have to choose which of these two categories you fall. My advice: take the halfway house and leave the prison in your rear view mirror.

What to Bring from Prison

So let's say you decided to take halfway house and you were given six months. In this chapter, we will discuss what you need to bring with you from prison to make your halfway house transition an easy one.

The B.O.P. has a contract with privately run halfway houses throughout the country. Each of these halfway houses are run a little differently, however there are rules that they are required to follow in accordance with B.O.P. policy.

I am going to describe my experiences in the halfway house I was sent to so just remember that each one is slightly different. My halfway house had dorm-style living, so each large dorm room housed approximately 65 residents.

Space is at a premium because the more individuals they can squeeze into these dorms, the more money they receive from the B.O.P. Just like prison, you will be given a bed (bunk beds only in my halfway house), a locker, and a chair.

So the first thing to bring with you from prison is your lock. If you don't, the halfway house is required to provide one, however, it may take a day or two before you receive it. In the meantime, anyone in your dorm will have access to the contents of your locker, so just a heads up.

You'll also want to bring several sets of socks and underwear, as well as a pair of shorts and maybe a sweat suit, depending on the time of year. We haven't discussed the pass system for halfway house yet, but you will be entitled to a pass soon after you arrive to go out and buy clothes and any necessary hygiene items. It may take a few days before you can leave the halfway house, so bring enough clothes and hygiene items to see you through.

If your family is coming to the prison to pick you up and drive you to the halfway house, they can bring clothes with them and you'll be all set. Your family can also send in a set of clothes to the prison for you to change into before you leave, that way you aren't walking through the gates in sweat pants.

So if you decide to take that option, you'll already have one set of clothes when you arrive at halfway house. Speak to your case manager about your prison facility's policy on mailing in clothes.

I brought a few books with me to halfway house because I didn't know how long I'd be there before being allowed to go out for the first time. It's nice to have something to read because most halfway houses don't have a library or a place to borrow books.

You won't need your radio to watch TV in halfway house, however, I still brought mine so I could listen to music. I would also consider bringing a few towels, a pair of shower shoes, and laundry supplies with you from prison.

When you arrive at the halfway house, a staff member will inspect all the items you are bringing in and let you know which are not allowed. The only thing they didn't allow me be bring in was a big duffle bag because they said it had too many zippers and would be too time consuming to inspect each time I came into the facility from the street.

Every time you return to the halfway house, either from a pass or from work, you will be patted down and your bag and any items on you will be searched. This is to prevent any contraband from entering the halfway house, such as drugs or weapons. You can have a backpack, but I would suggest waiting until you get to the halfway house before you purchase one.

Each halfway house has different policies concerning backpacks, their size, how many zippers/compartments, etc. Just wait until you arrive and see what other residents are using, then when you go out on a pass to buy things, you can shop accordingly.

One of the essential things I purchased soon after arriving was a mini DVD player with built-in screen. Again, wait on buying this until you go through orientation so you can find out if there are size restrictions. My halfway house limited the screen size to nine inches.

These are available at Wal-Mart or any retail outlet that sells electronics. It's great to be able to watch any movie you want any time of the day or night. Before I found a job and started working, I watched movies every evening to pass the time (and to catch up on the many episodes of Breaking Bad that I missed).

If you have family driving you to the halfway house and have asked them to bring some items you are unsure the halfway house will allow you to bring in, have a family member call the halfway house ahead of time. Simply have them ask whether that item(s) is permissible. You can get the halfway house's address and phone number from your case manager.

Halfway House Orientation

So you've arrived at the halfway house and are getting settled in – now what do you do? Well, usually within 24 hours of your arrival, you will be required to attend an orientation for new residents.

Oh, and by the way, you won't be referred to as an inmate any longer; you have now been promoted to the title of 'resident'. The first time I heard that term, I didn't know who they were talking about. I was so used to hearing about inmate so and so, it threw me for a loop.

The staff will also call you by your name, so for example, "How are you doing today Mr. Smith?". Quite a change from "What do you want inmate Smith!?". During orientation, you will learn the rules of the halfway house and what is expected of you.

The main thrust of halfway house is building accountability; the staff at the halfway house wants to make sure you can be trusted and that you are accountable for your actions. This is particularly important when you leave the halfway house to go on passes.

We will delve deeper into accountability and the pass system in the next chapter but for now, just know that orientation is your opportunity to be introduced to the rules and to ask questions.

As of this writing, Federal residents are allowed to have a cell phone, however, it can't be a smart phone and it can't have the ability to take pictures. Believe it or not, they still make cell phones with no camera.

If a family member or a friend is picking you up from prison to drive you to the halfway house, this is something they can give you so that you'll have the ability to communicate right away.

My advice is for your family to contact the halfway house ahead of time and ask them which type of phone is acceptable for Federal residents. The one my family purchased for me was a simple Tracfone, available at Wal-Mart or Target.

It's a pre-paid phone that does talk and text. You can have them go online or call to activate it, then all you have to do is buy minutes and you can load up the phone. The phone cards are sold everywhere and it takes less than a minute to add minutes to these phones.

The rumor is that the B.O.P. is considering allowing Federal residents to have a smart phone, although as of this writing, it hasn't happened yet. This would be a much-needed improvement, particularly when it comes to searching for jobs.

During orientation, you will receive several packets or information. One is the orientation manual specific to your halfway house. Another packet usually has information about local resources, such as local religious services, public transportation information, and things of that nature.

You will have your picture taken and be given an ID issued by the halfway house. This ID is your ticket out of the facility; without it, the staff will not allow you to leave the building. Keep it safe and don't lose it. Your halfway house ID will have your picture, your name, date of birth, inmate reg. number, date of issue, date of release from B.O.P. custody, as well as a bar code.

On the back of my ID, it had the name and address of the halfway house, in case you drop it on the street and someone finds it. That way, they can mail it back to you.

Unlike prison, you don't need your ID to get a tray of food, at least not in the halfway house I was assigned to. The main use for it is to check in and out of the facility. Also, during orientation, you will be given a tour of the facility.

You will learn where the laundry facilities are located, the cafeteria, the computer lab (if your facility has one), as well as the TV room, workout facilities, and outside recreation area.

If you are a smoker, you will not be permitted to smoke inside the halfway house, although you can smoke outside in the recreation area, as well as when you go out for passes.

One of the most important things you want to learn during orientation is where the blank passes are located, as well as where your case manager's mailbox is located. There will also be a place where you can check to confirm your upcoming passes –

find out where this is located as well. Here is a brief overview of each area of the halfway house.

Remember, your facility may be slightly different, but because these halfway houses are all contracted out from the B.O.P., they all have to follow similar rules and provide certain amenities to residents.

Cafeteria

The chow hall is very similar to Federal prison; you wait in line for a tray of mostly tasteless food high in sodium. They provide three meals a day, and you'll want to find out the approximate times for breakfast, lunch, and dinner. There will most likely be a weekly menu posted that lists each meal and what's on the menu for that particular day.

Ask at orientation to find out where this information is posted. If you miss a meal due to your work schedule, you will be provided with a bag lunch or the meal in a to-go container when you return. Make sure to ask about this once you start working.

The nice thing about halfway house is, if you don't want to eat what they are serving, the facility has a number of vending machines similar to what was in the visiting room in prison. Some of the common items available to you are soft drinks, sandwiches, snacks, ice cream, as well as coffee, tea, and hot chocolate. There will be a change machine as well.

Unfortunately, you cannot bring outside food into the facility. However, on Friday, Saturday, and Sunday evenings, as well as holidays, you can order take-out and have the food delivered to the halfway house. You'll see menus from local restaurants that deliver to the halfway house.

Ask at orientation if you can order from anywhere, or if there are approved businesses that you are limited to. I used to order take-out every Friday and Saturday night. Just pace yourself – remember, you haven't eaten this type of food for a while, so give your stomach a chance to adjust.

Dorms

The dorms where residents sleep are big rooms that house anywhere from fifty to one hundred residents. The beds are bunk beds, and each resident is assigned a locker and provided with a chair – just like in prison. I noticed that there was far less room to move around because they really had us all packed in there.

Remember, this is a business and these halfway houses receive money for each and every resident residing at their facility, so it's to their advantage to make effective use of the space.

Connected to the dorms are communal bathrooms, just like in prison, with a stretch of sinks, toilets, and shower facilities. The one difference from prison – they have mirrors. What a nice change from trying to shave with one of those cheap plastic mirrors they sell at commissary.

The same rules that applied in prison apply to halfway house concerning showering and bathroom usage. Be respectful, employ the "continuous flush" method I described earlier, and don't spend twenty minutes in the shower because there will be a line, and people actually have places to be (work).

Control Booths
I'm going to describe the set-up that my halfway house used for checking in and out of the facility, as well as checking your passes. In my facility, there were two "Control Booths", each staffed with people that work for the halfway house. There is someone in each of these control booths twenty-four hours a day.

Control Booth One handled checking residents in and out of the facility, as well as dealing with visitors and family members dropping off things for residents.

Control Booth Two is where you go to check your passes, pay your subsistence once you're working, as well as if you need to speak to a floor manager about something.

At each booth, they have a scanner that scans your ID card. That brings you up on their computer and then they can either check you out/in to the facility, or look up passes, or whatever else you need them to do.

Your facility may have a slightly different set-up so ask at orientation, especially during the tour so you know exactly where to go.

Outside Rec
Every halfway house is required to provide an outside recreation area to its residents. Depending

on the facility, you may have access to this area 24/7, or only at specific times during the day and evening.

My facility had picnic tables where residents would smoke, as well as two basketball nets and an area you could walk around. The outside rec area is fenced in so you can't just walk out and be on the street. The only way in and out of the facility is through a specific door.

Remember, you are still under B.O.P. custody. My facility had specified times that they would let us outside for rec. Ask during orientation how outside rec is handled and where the yard is located.

Case Manager Offices

When you first arrive at halfway house, you will meet with your assigned case manager – usually within the first twenty-four hours. Staff will have you sign some documents, find out a little about you and your goals, and help you formulate a plan for finding a job and eventually being released to your home on home confinement.

The first few weeks you will meet with your case manager once a week, then after that, twice per month. This is a great opportunity to ask them about their procedure for putting in passes, whether for work, religious services, or for social visits with friends and family.

They will show you how to submit your passes; most facilities have a mailbox for each case manager. You fill in the pass and deposit it in your case manager's box. They check their mailbox several times a day. If you get confused about how to fill out a pass, ask another resident.

TV & Workout Room

Each facility will have some sort of rec room where you can watch TV or workout. My facility had one room that housed both. There was a large flat screen mounted on the wall, as well as a workout area that included a pull-up bar, dip bar, and abdominal cruncher.

You won't need your radio to watch television; these TV's have the volume turned up. There was another TV in the cafeteria, and residents would hang out in there to watch television and eat out of the vending machines at night.

Now that we've taken a tour of a typical halfway house, let's talk about two vitally important things: accountability and the pass system that halfway houses utilize to allow residents to leave the facility for work, religious or social events.

Accountability

I want you to think of your halfway house experience as a test the B.O.P. is giving you. They are testing you to see if you'll comply with the rules and if you can be trusted out on the streets.

As I said before, this is a transition between prison and freedom, so you will get a taste, but you won't have complete freedom until you prove yourself. This is the focus of this chapter – how your halfway house measures accountability and how you can effectively manage their expectations and navigate the pass system they've put in place.

I remember the director of my halfway house telling us that he had only five rules he wanted us to follow. If we followed those five rules, we would have no problems with him or his staff. Those five rules were simple:

- No drinking alcohol
- No drugs
- If you're working, pay your subsistence on time
- Be where you say you're going to be
- Make sure to make your accountability calls

If you look at those five rules, they all center around one thing: **accountability**. You are accountable for your actions when at halfway house, and there are consequences if you break the rules. These are really very simple rules to follow, and if you are consistent with following them, your time will go quickly, the staff will begin to trust you, and you will be afforded opportunities to leave the halfway house more often on social passes. Let's go through the five rules one by one.

No Drinking

Just because you are outside the prison walls doesn't mean you can have a beer. You are still under B.O.P. custody, so until your official release date, you cannot drink alcohol. You might be asking yourself, "How will they know if I do?"

You will be required to take a Breathalyzer test each time you return to the halfway house from all passes. Do yourself a favor and just wait until you are finished with the B.O.P. before you decide to drink alcohol.

No Drugs

This is another one that is basic common sense. Whether you're in halfway house or on probation, you will not be allowed to take any illegal drugs or drugs that aren't prescribed to you. To keep you honest, you will be required to take a urine analysis (UA) once a week while at halfway house or on home confinement.

Pay Your Subsistence On-Time

When you start working, you will be required to give a percentage of that money back to the halfway house as a subsistence payment. Basically, now that you're working, you don't get free room and board anymore. As of this writing, the payment is steep – 25% of your pre-tax earnings. That's right – pre-tax. This means if you earn $1,000 a week before taxes, you'll be required to provide the halfway house with a money order for $250.

When you couple that with taxes, plan on taking home about half of what you earn while residing in the halfway house. But remember, once you go on home confinement, you won't be responsible for paying any subsistence.

Each halfway house has different procedures for subsistence payments and how they want the money. Most require a money order; no cash or personal checks. They will want a copy of your paystub along with the money order so they can make sure they are getting the full percentage.

Don't mess with subsistence payments and use a calculator just to make sure. If you are even fifty cents off, they will take away your social and work passes until you pay them what is owed.

Make copies of everything. I can't stress this enough because if a staff member messes up and they accuse you of not paying your subsistence on time or not paying what you owe, you can easily take out copies of everything and clear it up quickly.

I used to make copies of the money order I submitted, my paystub, and even the receipt the halfway house provided me. It's important to stay organized and keep your records in a safe place.

Be Where You Say You're Going to Be

Pretty self-explanatory – if you put in a pass to go to religious services and you decide instead to go to the movies, and you get caught, you will lose all your passes and have disciplinary actions taken against you. I saw this a lot with guys who would only pretend to go to work and they would instead head to their girlfriend's house.

The halfway house will randomly call your work to make sure you are there – if you're not, plan on meeting with the U.S. Marshalls when you arrive back at halfway house.

If the halfway house can't verify your location for more than two hours, that is considered an escape. What was intended as a quickie at your girlfriend's just turned into an escape charge. Just make it easier on yourself and go where you're supposed to go and don't deviate.

Accountability Calls

This is also a simple rule to follow, but you have to make it a habit. When you arrive at your destination, whether it be work, religious services, a job interview, or a social pass, you have to call the halfway house and tell them your name and that you have arrived at your destination.

When you leave that location, to either come back to the halfway house or to go to another location, you must call again to update your location. The tricky part about accountability calls is remembering to do them every time.

Sometimes, I would be in a rush and arrive at work a little late, and in that rush to get settled in and get started, I would forget to call. It only took one write-up before I made it a habit to pull out my cell phone and call.

One important note: don't erase the call records on your cell phone. There were three different occasions where I was written up for not making an accountability call but when I showed my case manager my cell phone and they could clearly see the exact time I called and the duration of the call, the write-up was thrown out.

Sometimes you need to hold the staff at the halfway house accountable too. The moral of the story is to use basic common sense and follow these five rules and your time at halfway house will be less stressful and more productive.

The Pass System

Types of Passes & Submitting Proof

Let's talk about the different types of passes and how often you are entitled to use them. The most common passes you will encounter are:

- Necessity pass
- Religious pass
- Grooming pass
- Goal pass
- Work pass
- Education pass
- Social pass

Necessity Pass

You are entitled to one (4) hour necessity pass each month. What exactly is a necessity pass? It's a pass that allows you to go shopping for necessities, such as clothing, shoes, cosmetics, and similar items. Those four hours you get include travel time, so prepare ahead of time a plan of action and look for stores that are close by your halfway house so you don't waste too much time traveling. Proof of a necessity pass is a copy of a receipt(s) from the stores you visited.

Religious Pass

You are entitled to one (4) hour religious pass each week, which includes travel time to and from the place of worship. Your halfway house should provide you with a list of local places of worship, categorized by faith, in your orientation packet. Proof of a religious pass is a church bulletin, flyer, or even a business card of the place of worship. Ask your case manager what is acceptable proof for your place of worship.

Grooming Pass

You are entitled to one (4) hour grooming pass each month, including travel time. This is your opportunity to get your hair cut, your beard trimmed, or any other type of grooming activity. Proof of a grooming pass is either a receipt or a business card from the business you visited.

Goal Pass

This pass may differ depending on your halfway house, but at mine, we were entitled to two (5) hour goal passes each month. A goal pass is a reward for achieving a goal you set out to accomplish.

When you meet with your case manager, he or she will ask you if you have any goals you are working on. They will enter that into the computer in your file, and when you achieve that goal (with proof), you will be able to put in a five-hour pass.

These passes are nice because you can go anywhere – to the movies, the mall, out to a restaurant. What type of goals are they looking for? Here are some suggestions:

- Acquiring your license or picture ID
- Setting up a bank account
- Acquiring health insurance
- Setting up a savings account
- Signing up for a class

You get the idea. Ask around at the halfway house and find out what other goals residents use to qualify for a goal pass.

Work Pass
This applies when you start working. You won't have to physically put in a pass everyday if your work schedule is consistent. You will initially put in a work pass for the days and times you are scheduled to work. Make sure to include travel time.

Halfway house rules state that you cannot be out of the halfway house on a work pass for more than fourteen hours in a row. Being that most jobs are eight hours a shift, plus two hours each way for travel time, the four teen hours should be plenty.

The proof that you were at work is your accountability call. The halfway house can call your employer at any time during your shift to make sure you are at work, as well as stop by for a quick visit.

Education Pass
This is a pass to allow you to leave the halfway house to go to a class. Most classes are approved if they are training-related classes that will help you acquire employment. If this is a one-time class, you will need to provide proof that you were there, like a flyer or some of the materials you were given relating to the class. If this is an on-going training, it is treated like your work pass and your accountability call will count as your proof.

Social Pass

This is the best pass of them all. These passes allow you to go to your home or your family and friend's homes to spend time with them. There are several varieties of social passes, with varying lengths of time, so let's discuss each one now.

- Six Hour Social Pass
- Eight Hour Social Pass
- Twelve Hour Social Pass
- Weekend Social Pass (48 hours)

The first three (six, eight, and twelve hour passes) are testing you to see how you do with accountability before the halfway house allows you to spend the night away from the facility. Those times include travel time as well.

Before you are able to go on any social passes, the home you will be visiting must have a basic phone line installed with only call waiting. No call forwarding is allowed. This way, you can't have all phone calls forwarded to a cell phone and then leave your home to get into trouble.

When you arrive at your home for a social pass, you must make an accountability call to your halfway house from the specific phone line you had installed. You let them know your name and that you have arrived for your social pass.

Staff at the halfway house can call you on that number at any time during your social pass, so make sure you are within earshot of the phone, or do what I did, and connect a wireless phone to the line and carry the phone around the house with you the whole time.

When you leave a social pass to come back to the facility, you must call from the same phone line and let them know you are on your way back. This is all about accountability. Don't forget to make your calls.

Once you have successfully completed several six, eight, and twelve-hour passes, you will be allowed to go on a weekend pass, which is forty-eight hours long. Same rules apply; make sure to make your accountability calls and have that phone close by at all times, even in the middle of the night.

Now that you've successfully completed all the social passes, if you are eligible, you will be released to home confinement. This is the ultimate goal for every halfway house resident. Each facility handles this process differently, so make sure to ask about all the requirements during orientation.

Job Hunting: Dealing with your Criminal Background

This is the final chapter of this section and a very important one. Many of you who are released from prison to your homes or a halfway house are not in a position to retire or just live off your savings. This means you will need to either go back to your old job or find a new one.

If you followed my advice earlier in this book and tried to create or maintain a good relationship with an employer prior to going into prison, then by writing to them six months before your release requesting to come back should put you in a good position concerning employment.

However, if this isn't the case then you will need to brush up on your job searching skills. The added challenge is that you will now be a felon, which can limit your job choices and eliminate other jobs that you may otherwise be well qualified to perform.

I am going to teach you some techniques and what to say during an interview to give you the best possible chance of acquiring a good job. The most important thing to remember is to be honest with any potential employer.

Don't lie with the hope that they won't do a background check and you'll be in the clear. That very well may happen, but eventually it will come out, then you will be at risk of losing the job and the reference you could have used to get a better job.

If you are searching for jobs while in the halfway house, there will be no way to avoid telling the employer you are a felon because the halfway house has to contact any potential employer before they give you a work pass. The first thing you need to think about is filling out the job application. Here are some questions to ask yourself:

- What classes, certifications, or skills did I acquire in prison that I can include on my job application or resume?
- Do I even need a resume?
- Will I need an email address, or just a phone number?
- What do I say when asked about my felony?

Let's break these questions down, one by one.

Classes, Certifications, & Skills

Again, if you followed the advice given in this book you will have taken plenty of A.C.E. classes and may even have received a certification in one or two areas. Which of these classes or certifications would apply to the job(s) you are applying for?

Some are obvious, like if you took classes in residential electric, this would absolutely apply to any job in construction. One of the certification classes I took was Lean Six Sigma, which is described as:

> "...a methodology that relies on a collaborative team effort to improve performance by systematically removing

waste and reducing variation. It combines lean manufacturing/lean enterprise and Six Sigma to eliminate the eight kinds of waste."

Now, how many employers would be thrilled with someone who can work collaboratively as a team and knows how to improve performance and remove waste?

This type of certification can be an asset to almost any employer – that's exactly why I decided to take the class! If you are reading this book before going to prison, you can see how important it is to plan out the classes and certifications you will take and not just take any class.

Do I need a resume?

The quick answer: YES! It's almost required for even the most menial of jobs, and it looks good to provide to every employer, even if they don't ask for one. My suggestion is to add the job(s) you worked in prison as well as any other job experience you had prior to prison.

One of the questions that many managers ask when interviewing is what jobs have you held in the last twelve to twenty-four months. You can include the jobs you worked in prison onto your resume.

As part of any basic resume, there is a section on education. In addition to any degrees and certifications you've received outside of prison, make sure to include any classes or certifications you completed while incarcerated.

Will I need an email address?

With technology moving as fast as it is, it's really a requirement now to have an email, as well as a phone number, included on your resume. Many jobs today only allow online applications and email is their preferred method of reaching out to you.

My suggestion is to go to Gmail and create a free email account. Try to acquire an email address that has your name included in the address. For example, if your name is Tom Smith, try to get something like: ThomasSmith@gmail.com or ThomasSmithemail@gmail.com.

What's nice about using your name in the address is it identifies you immediately and it's more professional than TDogg123@gmail.com.

Discussing your felony

No matter what your crime, there is a professional way to approach the topic and explain your mistake without excluding yourself as a candidate for the job. If you've ever been on a job interview, sometimes your potential employer will ask you to name one negative personality trait. In this situation, you need to learn how to pivot; shift the focus of the question while still answering it.

For example, if I were asked to name one of my negative personality traits, I might answer with:

> "I tend to take on too many responsibilities at work and get myself overwhelmed. I am working on focusing my attention on the important issues and completing them successfully before taking on more and

more tasks. In essence, I have been focusing more on quality than quantity."

Do you see how I took a negative and turned it into a positive? This is what we are going to have to do when being interviewed and questioned about our past as felons. We need to take responsibility for our actions but then show what we've learned and how we are now trying to improve ourselves.

Here is a script that works well on interviews that will help you take the negative connotation of "felon" and turn it into a positive learning experience and possible asset to a potential employer.

<u>Employer:</u> *I noticed that your last job was over five years ago. What have you been doing with yourself?*

<u>You:</u> "A few years ago, I made some mistakes and went away for a while; however, it was a pivotal moment in my life. It really changed me for the better. And the lessons I learned from that are incredible. And you know what? From that experience, I've gotten my life together. I'm extremely focused, driven, and hungry. I'm starting from scratch and I'm excited for the challenges and fresh opportunities ahead.

I'm telling you all this because I really like this restaurant - it seems like an awesome place to work, and I'd like you to give me the opportunity to be a part of your team. I'm a great (server, line cook) and I know I'll be an asset to you and your restaurant."

Here are some key points to remember:

- Don't be bitter
- Don't blame others or the system for your criminal history
- Be transparent, honest, and upfront about your past
- Acknowledge where you've been and where you're going

I'm not going to pretend that it's going to be easy to find that first job out of prison because it won't – it's going to be a challenge. It really comes down to a numbers game; where an ordinary citizen might have to go on three interviews to be offered a job, we as returning citizens might have to go on nine. Each interview you go on will sharpen your skills and give you good practice.

Don't get hung up on rejection or a potential employer coming across with a judgmental attitude. You are a strong and driven individual who has been through a lot. You survived and thrived in federal prison – you can certainly handle rejection. Just remember, when you finally land that job, it's going to feel so good and will be worth the struggle – trust me, I've been there!

Conclusion

My goal for publishing this little book was to provide soon-to-be released inmates with all the information they would need, not only survive their time in halfway house, but to thrive as well.

I also remembered how anxious I was before going to halfway house because there weren't any good resources to ease my anxiety and give me the knowledge I so desperately needed. I hope this small book serves that purpose for you.

Remember, knowledge is power – you now have the knowledge. Keep your spirits up, stay in touch with the people that love and care for you, and remember - you are almost there. I'll see you on the other side of the gates....

If you enjoyed this book, please leave me an honest review on Amazon– I'd love to hear from you.

http://surviventhrivebook.com/halfway

Made in the USA
San Bernardino, CA
16 September 2019